GOOD HOUSEKEEPING

QUILTING
AND
PATCHWORK

GOOD HOUSEKEEPING

QUILTING AND PATCHWORK

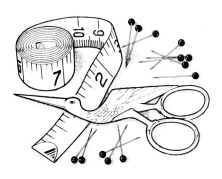

EBURY PRESS

Chief Contributor/Art Editor
Michele Walker

Editor
Melanie Miller

Good Housekeeping Quilting and Patchwork
was conceived, edited and designed by
Dorling Kindersley Limited, 9 Henrietta Street, London WC2E 8PS

First published in Great Britain in 1983 by
Ebury Press, National Magazine House,
72 Broadwick Street, London W1V 2BP

ISBN 0 85223 276 4

Printed in Singapore

Contents

Introduction   6

Basic Techniques   7

QUILTING

Wadded   20

Trapunto   32

Italian   34

PATCHWORK

Log Cabin   36

Strip   46

Repeated Blocks   56

Mosaic   66

Pictorial   74

Contemporary   82

Index   95

Introduction

Quilting and patchwork have always been two of the most popular needlecrafts and apart from being useful have fulfilled an important social role in women's lives. During the seventeenth and eighteenth centuries quilted clothes – especially hats, waistcoats and petticoats – became fashionable. Quilts and soft furnishings were also made from fine linens, silks and cottons, combining *Italian* and *Trapunto* quilting.

By the mid eighteenth century as fashions changed and more printed fabrics appeared, the finely worked plain quilts gave way to patchwork, which provided decorative articles more quickly.

Although the increased use of patchwork and later the introduction of commercially quilted fabrics led to an initial decline in hand quilting, the craft continued to flourish in certain areas: notably Durham, Yorkshire, Northumberland and South Wales. Isolation together with relative poverty and severe winters helped preserve the tradition.

During the nineteenth century quilting was part of many women's daily routine and a quilting frame, supported by four straight backed chairs was a familiar sight. Quilters were very proud of their work, most care and attention went to quilts made for their daughter's bottom drawer. However, everyday quilts were also needed that could be made economically and quickly. The north country *Strippy* was typical, consisting of unwanted strips of plain and printed fabrics filled with an old blanket or rags.

Quilting developed rapidly on both sides of the Atlantic during the nineteenth century but in America patchwork was more popular due to lack of fabric and the need to make warm bed covers quickly.

A social occasion was provided when the women got together in "quilting bees" to quilt the patchwork. The resulting quilts have now become collectors items and an established part of American Folk Art. Today the Amish communities in Pennsylvannia still support a strong quilting tradition and undertake to quilt contemporary designers' work, as well as their own traditional patterns.

Both quilting and patchwork have greatly increased in popularity during the last few years and are used for functional items, clothing and works of art. Quilts appeal to a wide range of people; makers, collectors or to those who just enjoy looking at them.

This book is aimed for all levels and is intended to stimulate the beginner, as well as the more experienced quiltmaker, to initiate explorations of their own.

BASIC TECHNIQUES

EQUIPMENT
Both quilting and patchwork require accurate craftsmanship and it is worthwhile investing in some good basic equipment.

For designing, making templates and marking fabrics.
Metal ruler, 2H pencil, coloured pencils, paper adhesive, graph paper, cutting knife, heavyweight card, tracing and note paper, set square, protractor, pair of compasses.
For sewing, quilting and tufting
Sewing and quilting thread, crochet cotton, sewing and quilting needles, lace pins, thimble, fabric scissors, small scissors, tape measure, quilting hoop or frame, iron and pressing cloth, sewing machine (optional).

FABRIC
Good quality, closely-woven dressweight cottons give excellent results for both quilting and patchwork and are easy to handle. Generally it is better to avoid synthetic, crease-resistant or stretchy fabrics. Tweeds, suitings and corduroys are suitable for large patches and machine sewing. Do not mix different weights of fabric together; the heavier weights pull and tear the lighter ones. For a project that is to be laundered, wash fabrics before use to test for shrinkage and colour fastness. When hand quilting select a fabric that is easy to sew and in a plain, light colour to show the stitches. Lawn, poplin, brushed cotton, silk and satin are all suitable. For backing quilting and patchwork choose a plain or printed cotton fabric.

WADDING
The most popular waddings are the light-weight, washable synthetic types. Choose the thinner, 2oz weight for hand quilting and the thicker 4oz or 8oz for tufting. Alternative waddings are cotton domette, woollen domette which has an open knitted texture, and the old fashioned dense cotton wadding. These last three waddings produce a flatter effect but give more weight to a project which makes them suitable for wall-hangings. They are excellent for machine quilting and easy to handle, but should be dry cleaned.

Lawn

Cotton

Brushed cotton

Silk

Corduroy

Tweed

Synthetic wadding

Cotton domette

Woollen domette

Cotton wadding

Quilting

WADDED QUILTING

Quilting can be worked by hand or machine. The stitches are sewn uniformly over three layers of fabric: top, wadding and backing, in order to keep them together.

DESIGN

Before starting a design consider the item on which it is being applied. Symmetrical designs are suitable for cushions and quilts, asymmetrical designs are better for clothes, curtains and bags. Traditional designs are best made from a collection of templates arranged in an overall pattern consisting of a border and corner motifs linked to a dominant centre with background, or small filler patterns.

Whatever the design, it is important to have a variety of contrasting shapes and textures, and to carefully work it out on graph or tracing paper before marking the fabric. Avoid small, intricate motifs which are difficult to work, especially for machine quilting; here the design needs to be bold and simple. When quilting patchwork the stitching can either outline the patches or make contrasting shapes and textures.

Symmetrical

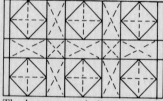

The shapes are evenly distributed to give a balanced design.

Asymmetrical

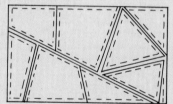

The shapes are unevenly distributed to give an irregular design.

CUTTING THE LAYERS

Cut the three layers slightly larger than the required size - quilting tends to shrink the work, as much as 10cm on large quilts. If the top and backing fabrics need to be made up from several widths, avoid a centre seam. Place a complete width of fabric in the centre with a half width added to each side. To join widths of wadding into a larger piece, butt and stitch together.

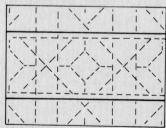

Make side seams that do not interrupt the centre design.

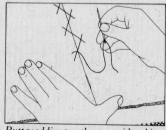

Butt wadding together to avoid making a ridge.

MARKING THE FABRIC

It is much easier to mark the design on the top fabric (right side) before assembling the layers together. There are several ways of transferring the design, but first lightly press the top fabric into quarters to mark the centre point and main divisions in the area to be filled.

Templates

Templates are simple outline shapes and can be bought, or made from card. Place one right side up on the fabric and mark around the edge with a coloured pencil. Add the inside lines freehand. A template is needed for each individual shape.

Use a long ruler to mark filler patterns.

Needle marking

Place the fabric on a padded surface before marking with a blunt ended needle. Hold the needle almost parallel to the fabric and press down to form an indented line.

Transparent fabrics

If the fabric is slightly transparent place the completed design underneath and trace off with a well sharpened coloured pencil.

Guide the needle against a template.

Dressmaker's carbon

For more opaque fabrics place the design right side up on the right side of the fabric. Place carbon paper carbon side down in between and draw over the design with a well sharpened 2H pencil.

USING A HOOP

It is advisable to use a hoop or frame for quilting to keep the layers together and evenly stretched. A large hoop requires less space than a frame, is portable and suitable for any size work. Avoid leaving the work in a hoop unworked for a long period as this tends to mark the fabric.

Preparing the layers

Assemble the three layers on a flat surface, first the backing fabric wrong side up, then the wadding, and finally the top fabric right side up. Smooth out any wrinkles. It is important to tack the layers thoroughly together. Put the work in the hoop right side up so that it is evenly stretched but has enough give to enable several stitches to be taken at once. Check the back to make sure it is flat and smooth. Start in the centre of the work and progress outwards. Rest the hoop on the edge of a table so that both hands are free to quilt.

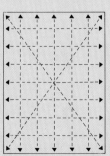

Start at the centre and tack outwards.

USING A FRAME

Traditionally quilts were made on a frame and, although it requires more space than a hoop, there are several advantages: the work can be left set up for long periods; it requires less tacking and handling; and several quilters can work on one project at the same time. A frame has two long rails, each with webbing attached, and two stretchers. The rails have a slot at each end through which a stretcher is put and held in place with a peg. The frame must be free-standing or supported so that both hands are free to quilt.

Preparing large items

Sew only the backing fabric to the webbing on each rail. Roll the surplus around the top rail, leaving about 40cm (16in) exposed. Add the stretchers. Lay first the wadding, then the top, right side up over the backing. Tack layers along the bottom edge and allow the extra fabric and wadding to hang over the top rail. Tape the sides. Start sewing from the bottom edge and work across. As the work progresses unroll the backing on the far rail and roll the completed area around the bottom rail. Continue until the quilting is complete.

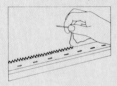

Herringbone stitch the backing fabric to each runner.

Loop tape over stretcher to secure each side and pin through all layers.

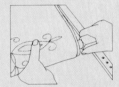

Remove tapes and pins before rolling the finished area of work on.

Preparing small items

Stitch several lines of tacking to keep the three layers together. Sew the top and bottom edges of the work right side up to the webbing on each rail. Roll the surplus around each rail to expose the centre area. Add the stretchers then secure the sides with tape. The work should be held flat and evenly secured, but the tension kept springy. As the work progresses wind on a new area.

HAND STITCHING

Thread a short length of quilting cotton and knot the end that's cut to prevent the thread from twisting. Start in the centre of the work and pull the thread through to the top from the back so that the knot is held beneath the wadding. Make a small, evenly spaced running stitch; the work should be reversible. To finish the quilting make a knot close to the last stitch and pull the thread through to the back so that the knot is again caught under the wadding; cut thread.

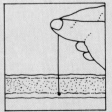

Give the thread a gentle pull to bring knot under wadding.

10

Positioning the hands

The sewing hand should be on the top guiding the needle through with a thimble on the middle finger. Keep the thumb pressed down just ahead of the stitching. The other hand should be below the work to feel the needle come down and to guide it back up. As the work progresses a rhythm is obtained making it easier to work small even stitches.

Take several stitches at once.

FINISHING

There are several ways to finish the edges but first remove the work from the hoop or frame. The simplest method of finishing is to turn both fabric edges to the inside, trim wadding back and work two rows of running stitch through all layers.

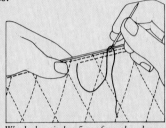

Work the stitches 5mm from the edge.

Piped edge

Piping gives a neat firm edge to the work. Cover piping cord with bias strips in a contrasting colour or cut from top fabric. Attach the cord, right sides and raw edges together, to the front of the work, then turn to inside. Turn under the raw edge of the backing fabric, tack in position then carefully slip stitch to the piping.

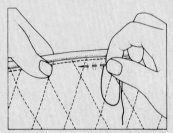

To secure backing to cord use slipstitch or two rows of running stitch.

TUFTING

If larger patchworks are not quilted the backing and wadding tends to wrinkle and drop. Tufting or tying with a heavy crochet cotton is a quick and effective way of keeping the three layers together. Do not use a synthetic thread because it will not hold in a knot. The tufts can be in colours to match the ground fabric and worked in the seam line, or decorative in different colours.

Make one stitch through layers leaving a long end. Make a second stitch at the same point.

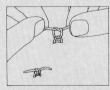

Tie ends together, right over left, left over right. Do not pull too tightly.

Trim ends. The tufts can be made on the front or back of the work.

11

MACHINE QUILTING

Machine quilting produces a harder line and is more suited to contemporary work. Pin the layers together and quilt the design from the centre outwards. Stitch the lines in opposite directions to prevent the layers slipping. Use a medium length stitch and slightly loosen the tension to make sewing easier.

A guide attachment avoids marking the lines.

TRAPUNTO AND ITALIAN QUILTING

Trapunto and Italian quilting use only two layers of fabric stitched together with a filling or cord inserted between to raise the surface.

Fabrics and fillings

The top fabric should be fine and closely woven, use cotton or silk and the backing fabric loosely woven such as mull. Use Kapok filling inserted with a crochet hook for Trapunto work and quilting or Aran knitting wool threaded with a blunt ended needle for Italian quilting.

Trapunto quilting

Mark the design on the backing fabric.

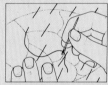

Tack the top and backing fabrics together.

Stitch the design through both layers.

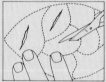

Make small slits in backing fabric.

Insert padding with crochet hook.

Slipstitch the slits to close.

Italian quilting

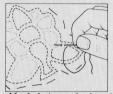

Mark design on back and stitch along the double lines.

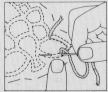

Ease threads open and insert wool from the back along channels.

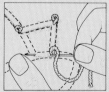

At sharp curves bring needle out and loop cord to stop puckering.

Patchwork

Before a patchwork pattern is chosen, you should first decide what you want to make, its size and whether you want to sew it by hand or machine. There are three methods of sewing patchwork: first by machine, which gives the strongest results and is particularly good for heavier fabrics; second by hand, using a small running stitch – this is how most traditional American patchworks were made – and, thirdly, by hand, using paper templates. This last method, which takes the longest time, gives very accurate results and is usually associated with traditional English patchwork.

SIZE

For a beginner, smaller items such as cushions, cot quilts or wall-hangings, are good projects to try. They will enable you to become familiar with patchwork techniques without being overwhelmed by size. When making a cushion cover, buy the pad first and make the cover 25mm (1in) smaller – a patchwork cushion cover looks best when it is a tight fit. To estimate the size of a patchwork bedcover, drape a sheet over the bed and take the measurements from it. In this way you will be able to estimate the size required to cover the pillows and blankets, and to calculate the overhang.

CHOOSING A PATTERN

Once you have decided on the project and its size you can then start choosing a pattern. Pick one that both interests you and fits your purpose. Try and relate it to the size of the finished piece – it is important that the individual pieces should not be too small and difficult to sew, or so large that they look clumsy and out of scale on the finished project. Patterns that have large repeats, such as *Garden maze*, cannot be reduced easily and are not suitable for small projects. Seminole patchwork, on the other hand, is more versatile and can easily be adapted for use on large or small quilts, or for decorating clothes.

The amount of time you have available is also an important consideration: some patterns, such as *Honeycomb*, are best made by hand using papers, and take much longer than, say, *Log cabin*, which can be made quickly with a machine.

The repeated block patterns offer the most design possibilities because when the blocks are set together patterns emerge which are not obvious from looking at a single block. The blocks can also be set diagonally.

DESIGN

Before sewing, work out size, pattern colours and textures. If the design is based on a repeated block, trace off any pattern from this book and colour it in. Try several colour variations, then put four blocks together – straight block-to-block setting gives the most potential for pattern-making. As you become more familiar with traditional quilt patterns you will see that most blocks fit into a grid (the number of squares into which a block can be divided). Four-, five-, seven-, and nine-patch are the most common. This grid system will give a good idea of how the block is put together.

13

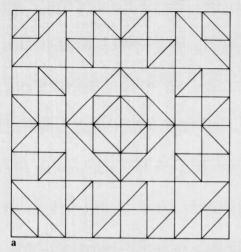

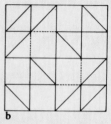

a *Four* Double X *blocks give a pattern not apparent from looking at a single block.*

b *A 4-patch pattern can be divided into 4 squares, or multiples of 4.*

While it is important for the scale of the block to suit the size of project, when using traditional patterns it is not always possible to work to a set size because block patterns tend to be squares of 20-30cm (8-12in). Generally, a pattern made from a number of smaller blocks is more interesting than one which uses only a few over-sized blocks. To incearse the area of patchwork, without making extra blocks, alternate the pieced blocks with squares of printed or plain fabric. The size can also be increased by setting the blocks with lattice strips which also act as good harmonizers of colours in a scrap quilt. Borders are also useful because they help make the patchwork fit a required size and also frame the work.

One-patch patterns do not have as many variations as block designs but it is still important to plan first. It is a good idea to divide the fabrics first into colour categories, before assembling the patches. Then make the final arrangement before sewing.

Finally, it is important to make a scale drawing. This will show the relative size of the patterns and is useful for determining borders. You can easily estimate how many templates are needed and the number of patches from each colour. This drawing is an invaluable guide for making up the patchwork.

TEMPLATES

Once the design has been chosen, the templates can be made. These must be accurate because they are the patterns from which each shape is cut out in a given design. An error in size, however slight, will compound to several centimetres over an entire piece of work.

Templates should always be cut from a strong material that will keep its shape, such as mounting card. Medium-weight sandpaper is also ideal and it has the added advantage of adhering to the fabric. Many of the geometric shapes used in patchwork can be drawn from graph paper, then cut out and stuck on mounting card or sandpaper.

Cutting templates from square and isometric paper

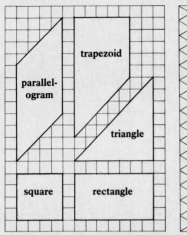

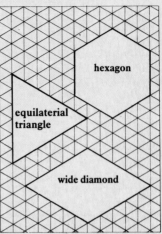

There are two diamond shapes which are commonly used in patchwork: the 60°–120° diamond, used for six-pointed stars and hexagons, (this can be cut from the triangular grid graph paper); and the long 45°–135° diamond, used for eight-pointed stars, which has to be drawn with a set square and a pair of compasses.

Constructing the long diamond

Draw AB. Using a protractor or set square draw AC at 45° from AB making it the same length as AB. With the compass point on C, make an arc. With the point on B, make another arc to cut the first one at D. Join BD and CD.

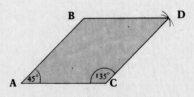

Templates for machine sewing

The size of these includes the finished size of the patch plus a seam allowance of 6mm (¼in) or 9mm (⅜in). Whatever size seam allowance is chosen, it must remain consistent throughout.

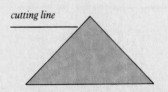

Templates for hand sewing without papers

These are window templates (empty frames). The inner edge represents finished size of the patch and is the sewing line. The outer edge is fabric cutting line. Give these templates a firmer marking edge by making seam allowance 9mm (⅜in).

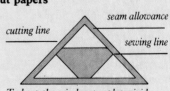

To keep the window template rigid, leave the central area uncut.

Templates for hand sewing with papers

Three templates are needed: one made 6mm (¼in) bigger on all sides (used for cutting the fabric); the second made to the exact size of the finished patch (used for backing papers), and the third is a window template for patterned fabrics, the same size as the first template (used for framing the printed fabric).

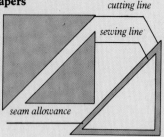

cutting line

sewing line

seam allowance

ESTIMATING THE FABRIC

Unless you are making a patchwork from scraps it is important to estimate accurately the amount of fabric needed. This can only be done when all templates are cut and the number of pieces is known.

Always include seam allowances when estimating fabric. The width of fabric is usually 90cm (36in) or 115cm (45in). See how many times the template can be laid across the width. For example, if using fabric 90cm (36in) wide, and a template 8cm (3¼in) square you will get eleven squares to a width. To estimate the length of fabric needed, divide the number of squares required by the number of times a template fits across the width of fabric and multiply the result by the width of the template. So, if you need one hundred squares, calculate thus: $100 \div 11 \times 8$cm (3¼in) = 72cm (29in). It is advisable to add a little extra so, in this case, 90cm (36in) of fabric would be adequate. Borders and lattice strips are estimated in the same way, using the width of the fabric as a basis of measurement.

MARKING AND CUTTING THE FABRIC

Fabric for patchwork is always marked on the wrong side with a well-sharpened pencil. It is a good idea to use a dark-coloured pencil for light fabrics and a light colour for dark fabrics.

When placing the template on the fabric, align the sides with the straight- or cross-grain where possible, avoiding the bias of the fabric, which has most stretch. Fit the templates flush together.

Some patchwork shapes, such as the trapezoid, have definite right and wrong sides and are not reversible like the square or the rectangle. When cutting these non-reversible shapes, place the template wrong side up on the wrong side of the fabric.

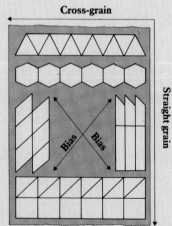

Cross-grain

Straight grain

Bias *Bias*

The selvedge edges run parallel to the straight grain which has minimum stretch.

SEWING

When you are ready to start sewing, lay out all the patchwork shapes in the correct order so that you can check the pattern for any mistakes and view the design as a whole. Not all hand sewing can be done by machine so it is useful to know both techniques, but two principles apply to both. First, use straight seams and avoid sewing into corners. Second, it is much easier to join the smallest pieces into progressively bigger units until the patchwork is complete. The technique is illustrated below, in this case for the *Sherman's march* block.

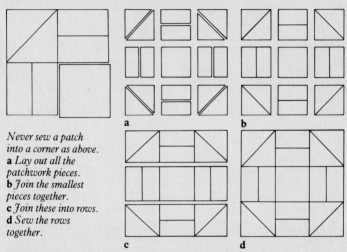

Never sew a patch into a corner as above.
a *Lay out all the patchwork pieces.*
b *Join the smallest pieces together.*
c *Join these into rows.*
d *Sew the rows together.*

Machine sewing

This is the quickest method of making patchwork and is suitable for all shapes that are not too small (less than 4cm [1½in]). Set the machine to about five stitches per centimetre (twelve per inch). Choose a needle size suitable for the fabric being sewn and use cotton polyester thread. The patches must be accurately cut because in machine sewing the edge of the fabric is aligned against the edge of the presser foot which usually determines a seam allowance of 6mm (¼in). On some machines it may be easier to align the fabric with the seam allowance incised on the plate below the foot. If your machine does not have an indicator use masking tape.

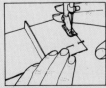

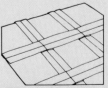

Align edge of fabric with presser foot. Start and end with a back stitch; remove pins before sewing.

Press seams open. When sewing matching seams together, pin either side of seam.

When machine patchwork is complete press all seams open. First press on back and then front.

Hand sewing without papers

Use No. 8 Sharp needles and, if possible, quilting thread which is the strongest. If this is not available, use a waxed cotton-covered polyester. Strands should be no longer than 40cm (16in) and remember to knot the end you cut to prevent twisting. Always mark hand sewn patches on the wrong side of the fabric and never sew through the seam allowance.

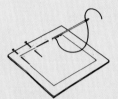 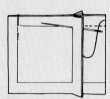 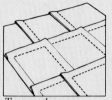

With patches right sides facing pin and match pencil lines. Sew with running stitch, ending with a back stitch.

Join rows of patches by first pinning them at corresponding seams. Next sew along matching pencil lines.

To strengthen seams press to one side – usually the darkest side – or, to avoid lumpiness, alternate the direction.

Hand sewing with papers

This method gives very accurate results and is used for patterns which mainly contain geometric shapes such as hexagons and diamonds although it works equally well with a block design. The fabric is tacked over the paper templates, then the individual patches are overstitched together into rows and the rows formed into larger units. The papers are removed when the patchwork is complete.

 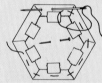 

Lay patch right side down and pin a paper template to centre. Fold fabric edge over and secure with tape.

Tack all round the patch and carefully remove the masking tape.

Press the fabric folds – this makes sewing the patches much easier.

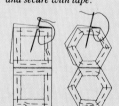 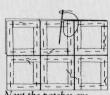 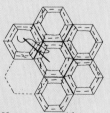

Individual patches are first joined with tiny overcasting stitches.

Next the patches are joined into rows, with overcasting stitches.

Hexagons can either be joined in rows or formed into rosettes.

BORDERS

Before a border is added, the patchwork should be pressed. Use a cloth to prevent glazing and iron on the back and then the top. Borders can be plain or they can be a contrasting pattern to the patchwork. They are either used as a frame or they can be used to increase a patchwork's size. Either way, they should be planned as part of the patchwork as a whole. The seams should correspond with the seaming of the patchwork and the dimensions must correspond accurately. See below for three different methods for joining borders.

Four-patch border

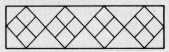

Navajo border

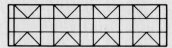

Arrow border

Zigzag border

Straight cut

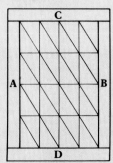

Add A and B (they are same length as patchwork). Now add C and D (width of patchwork plus A and B).

Mitred

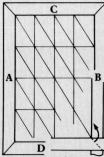

Cut A and B, also C and D to required size. Fold back diagonally at each corner as shown.

Separate corners

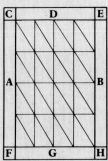

Cut A and B to required size. Join C, D, E and F, G, H into 2 separate strips. Join to patchwork.

EDGING AND LINING

Large patchworks, when finished, need to be lined both to neaten and to strengthen them – and dress-weight cotton is best for this purpose. There are two ways of applying a backing fabric. The first is to cut it the same size as the patchwork and make a separate binding for the edge. The binding can be sewn on in the same order as the straight-cut border, then folded over to the back and hand stitched into position. The second method is to cut the backing fabric 25mm (1in) larger than the top on all sides and bring it over to the front of the patchwork to make a self-binding.

WADDED

*The earliest type of quilting
was made for protection but later used primarily
for warm bed covers and clothing. The quilting stitch which
holds the two layers of fabric and a filling together gives texture
to a plain surface or can be used together with patchwork.
Wadded quilting designs can be random or decorative,
and a comparison between North country
and Welsh quilts illustrates the regional
development of patterns.*

North country

English cot quilt, Durham 1930s Pale grey silk, white silk backing and cotton wool wadding. Quilted with a central design of roses, shells and leaves and a border of feathers and roses.

Materials Choose natural fibres, closely-woven cottons, silk or fine linen in light shades.
Uses Christening or special quilt for a baby.

**Running feather border
with corner rose and shell motifs**

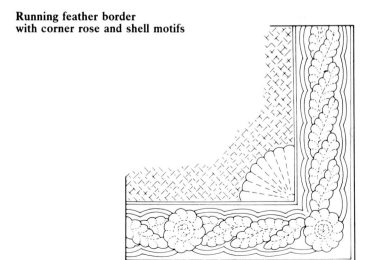

Basket

Early twentieth-century English quilt Patchwork quilt of white and pink cotton illustrating a basket pattern with appliqué handles. The quilting pattern has been made to fit the patchwork and shows scroll and flower motifs with a linked diamond and chain type border. It was marked by Elizabeth Sanderson, and the pattern was quilted by Deborah Adamson of County Durham in 1912.

Materials Plain coloured, good quality dress-weight cottons.
Uses Set together on a quilt or singly for cushions or bags.

Construction Make up the basket blocks and frame each one with a plain strip. Set diagonally with plain squares before adding the border.

Basket block

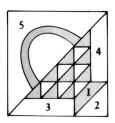

First sew the small triangles together, then add the remaining shapes 1-4 and 5. Turn under the raw edges of the basket handle and position. Appliqué with a small overcast stitch.

Overcast stitch

Border and corner square

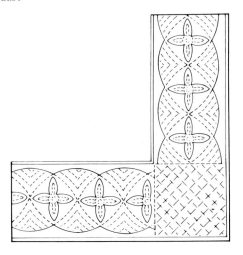

Feathers, leaves and shells

English quilt 1930 Detail from a typical North country quilt, illustrating a border of curved feather, rose and leaf motifs set against a diamond filler pattern.

Materials Use a fabric with a lustre to emphasize the quilting pattern: cotton, poplin or silk are all suitable.
Uses The motifs can be used singly or repeated in a border.

Feathers

Leaves

Shells

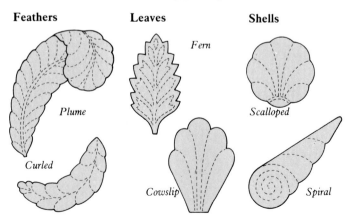

Plume

Curled

Fern

Cowslip

Scalloped

Spiral

Circles, fans and hearts

Welsh quilt 1920 Detail from a typical Welsh quilt showing the characteristic spiral or snail pattern. Many of the motifs found on these quilts also decorate Welsh love spoons.

Materials Good quality washable cotton fabric.
Uses The motifs can be set together in various sizes, used as focal points or to fill corners.

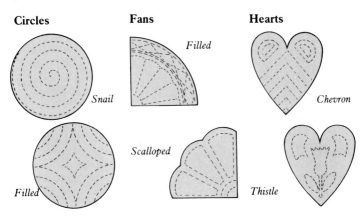

Circles

Snail

Filled

Fans

Filled

Scalloped

Hearts

Chevron

Thistle

Borders and fillers

Uses As a continuous line around the design or in combination with corner motifs.

Uses As a background worked uniformly over the quilt or to link individual motifs.

Scalloped

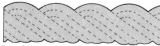

Lined

Feather

Linear

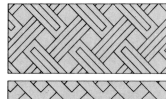

Diamond chain

Plaited chain

Undulating

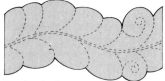

Running feather

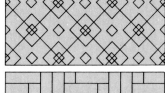

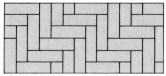

Crescents

Cord and tassel

Hammock

Circular

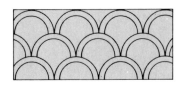

Repeated motifs

Uses Composite shapes made from individual motifs and used for central designs or to fill corner squares on large quilts. Link the motifs together with a filler pattern.

Shells

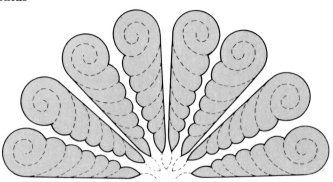

Feathers

Hearts

Wedding

Welsh wedding quilt 1888 by Mary Williams of Monmouthshire made from cotton fabric with wool wadding. The design has a large centre circle with a heart in the middle and this is repeated on a smaller scale in each corner. Shells, fans, Welsh pears (paisley), spirals, tulips and large leaf motifs are also illustrated.

Materials Good quality cotton, linen or silk
Uses Wedding quilt or use individual motifs for cushions, or nightdress case or hot water bottle cover.

Tulip

Welsh pears

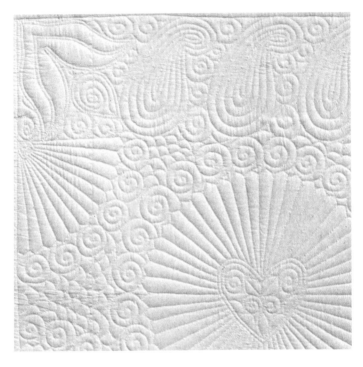

**Border with leaf
and circular motifs**

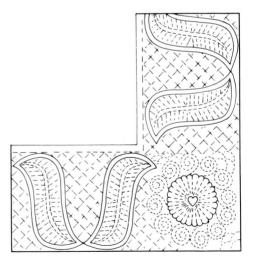

Welsh

Welsh quilt made by Mary Thomas of Carmarthenshire, illustrating a large central design with a rose, tulips and leaves which are repeated in the border. The separate corner squares show an arrangement of four hearts, each filled with spiral motifs.

Materials Closely-woven cotton poplin or silk.
Uses Large quilt or use individual motifs for waistcoat, dressing gown, or border around a skirt.

Rose   **Tulip**   **Leaf**

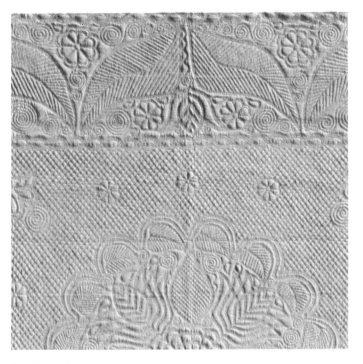

Border and corner square

TRAPUNTO

Here the technique is used decoratively
to give emphasis to enclosed solid areas within a design.
The outline of a shape is stitched through two layers of fabric
and a padding is inserted from the back of the work.
Trapunto can be combined with other types of
quilting or appliqué and is also known
as stuffed quilting.

Flower garland

Detail of American trapunto quilt 1850 Handsewn by Mrs Garhart, made from cotton fabric with a cotton filling. In 1866 it won 'Best White Quilted Bedspread' in the Agriculture Society Show, Albany County.

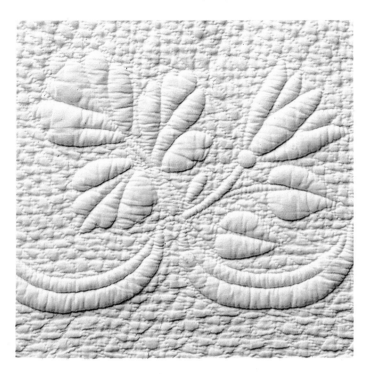

Materials Fine linen, lawn or silk
Uses Quilt, soft furnishings, evening jacket, decorative purse or bag.

**Central design
of flowers and leaves**

ITALIAN

*This is mainly used for decoration
and in combination with other types of quilting or patchwork.
Linear patterns are made by stitching two layers of fabric
together in narrow parallel lines and threading a cord
through from the back to raise the surface.
The lines can be continuous or interlacing,
set solid or used singly to outline a shape.
It is also known as cord quilting.*

Pastel Squares

Child's cot quilt 1976 made up from a number of individual squares combining both patchwork and Italian quilting.

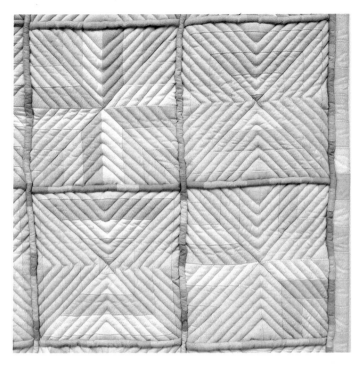

Materials Plain, light coloured, closely-woven cotton fabrics for the squares, with darker shades for the outlining piped strips.
Uses Large and small quilts, soft furnishings and wall-hangings.

Construction First make up the patchwork squares. Mark the same quilting design on all the backing squares. Quilt each square individually. Join small strips of fabric into lengths to cover the piping cord. Join the quilted patchwork squares into vertical strips with a covered length of piping cord (cut to the width of the square) in between. Join the vertical strips together with long lengths of covered piping cord cut to size. Add a separate strip border and backing to complete.

Typical patchwork square and quilting pattern

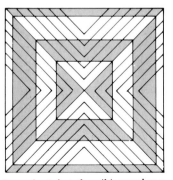

Remember to loop the quilting wool at a sharp angle to avoid puckering the fabric.

LOG CABIN

Log cabin is the most well known of all patchwork patterns and shows the skillful ingenuity of the early quiltmakers. The block is usually divided diagonally into a light half and a dark half, and is made from strips sewn around a centre square. The pattern is very easy to make, requires only one template for the centre square, and the blocks can be arranged in many ways to give a variety of designs.

Chequerboard

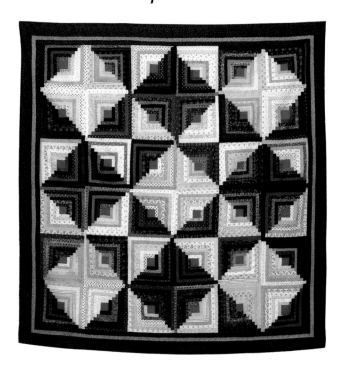

A contemporary patchwork quilt using a variety of fabrics including a selection of dark prints bought from French street markets which are traditionally made up into work dresses and aprons. This unusual setting of the *Log cabin* blocks creates a chequerboard effect.

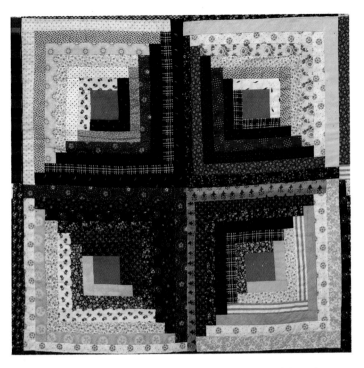

Materials Use contrasting cotton fabrics in dark and light prints.
Uses Suitable for a quilt, wall-hanging, curtains or cushions.

Construction
see p.38

Lay out all the completed blocks in the correct position before sewing together.

Arrangement of blocks

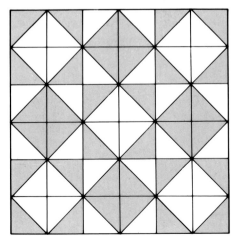

Straight furrow

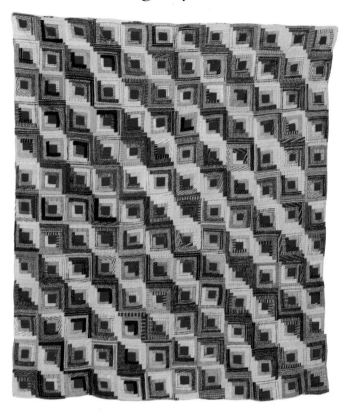

Late nineteenth-century American patchwork quilt Good use has been made of left over scraps of shirting fabrics.

Materials Denim and corduroy for wide strips, shirting fabrics for narrower ones.

Uses Make one large block for a cushion or twelve smaller blocks for a cot quilt.

Construction To make one block take a light coloured strip, align edge with the top edge of the centre square right sides facing and sew together. Trim strip to width of square and press back to right side. Attach second light strip and cut to the length made by the previous strip and square.

Log cabin block

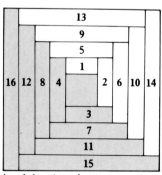

Attach the strips to the centre square in a clockwise progression.

Change to the dark colour and add the third and fourth strips to complete the first round. Continue in this way, always keeping the lights and darks in the same position until the block is completed.

Arrangement of blocks

Unlike some designs using the Log cabin *blocks, the* Straight furrow *arrangement is suited to both large and small quilts. Position the blocks so that the light and dark fabrics make strong diagonal lines across the quilt.*

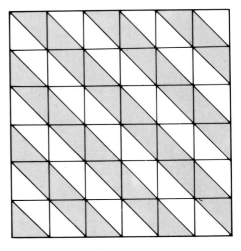

Barn raising

A contemporary patchwork quilt using an off-centre *Log cabin* block arranged in a pattern called *Barn raising*.

Materials Combine cottons with more lustrous fabrics such as silks, satins or taffetas.

Uses The block is easy to sew and suitable for making a large quilt or wall hanging.

Construction Use the same technique as described for the block on p.38 but attach the strips on two sides only.

One block

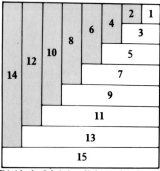

Divide the fabric into lights and darks and join the strips in the above sequence.

Arrangement of blocks

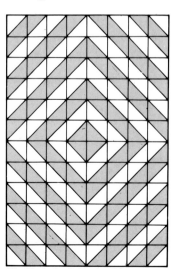

The blocks in the Barn raising *pattern make an expanding diamond shape.*

Border Use one plain fabric combined with similar strips used in the main patchwork. Make up the border blocks and link together with strips of fabric. Attach the border as for separate corners, see p.19

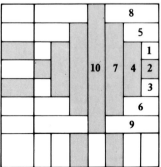

Join the strips in the above sequence and repeat for each side.

Courthouse steps

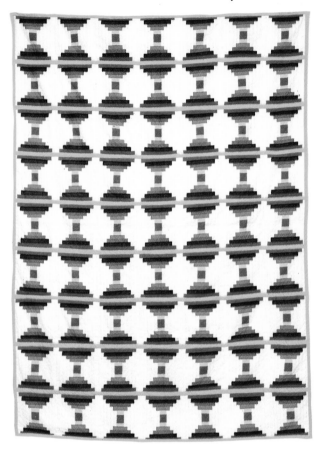

A modern quilt using the traditional *Courthouse steps* pattern in strong, vibrant colours. Each block is divided into quarters with the same colour repeated in the opposite strip to make an hourglass shape.

Materials Choose cotton fabrics in plain bold colours or prints for a softer effect.

Uses All the *Log cabin* patterns are good for beginners and are easily adapted to small items such as placemats, cushions and bags.

Construction This block is made in a similar way to all previous blocks which use the strips already sewn as a cutting guide line. Attach the first strip, then add the second strip using the same colour on the opposite side of the square. Change colour and add the third and fourth strips, one to each side to complete the first round. Continue adding strips, first to the top and bottom, then to the sides, until the block is finished.

Attach the strips in the order shown and remember to press each one back to the right side before sewing adjoining strips. The blocks can either be set solid or the rows joined together with a narrow horizontal band.

Courthouse steps block

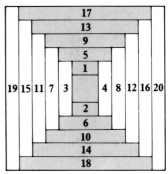

Pineapple

Nineteenth-century American patchwork quilt Both machine and hand stitching have been used in this bold design. The pineapple was a symbol of hospitality in colonial America and the shape frequently appeared on gateposts. The block is also known as *Maltese cross*.

Materials The pineapple block is more intricate than the previous patterns; use closely-woven, good quality cottons that press well.
Uses The size gradation of strips makes it an interesting block to use on its own; set four or more together for a wall-hanging.

Construction This block requires a template for each different size strip as well as the centre square. It is best to enlarge the block on graph paper, cut out each shape and stick on card, adding a 6mm (¼in) seam allowance to each edge before cutting out. Begin by adding a small triangle to each side of the centre square so that it is set on its point. Add a small dark strip to each side then a light coloured strip to complete the first round. Continue in this way adding progressively longer strips, first the dark then the light and finally completing the square with a large triangle in a different colour at each corner.

The blocks can be sewn by hand or machine. Unlike the previous Log cabin patterns each strip must be cut to the required length before sewing.

Pineapple block

STRIP

*This technique describes patchwork
that is made up from strips of fabric rather than blocks or
repeated shapes. The basic Strippy originated in north-
east England and is the simplest type of patchwork
made from long lengths of fabric cut to the size of
the quilt. Strip patterns also include Seminole
patchwork where the strips are sewn
together, cut, and resewn to create
intricate patterns.*

Strippy

English quilt 1870 made by Elizabeth Womphrey, in Wallsend. The
strippy was a popular pattern for everyday quilts and although the
patchwork was simple to make the plain panels provided an
opportunity to quilt elaborate patterns.

Descent into tranquility

A contemporary wall-hanging made from a wide range of fabrics in contrasting tones and textures.

Materials Cottons, fine wools, corduroys and silk (use doubled for durability).
Uses Warm bed quilt, or wall-hanging.

Construction The strips are joined and quilted in one operation. Grade fabrics into lights and darks and make up long strips to the width of the quilt. Arrange in a V-shape design. Cut backing and wadding to the size of the finished quilt and tack together. Using the tacking as a guide for positioning the strips, pin the centre strip in position right side up, take the next strip and place face down on the first strip. Sew across thus joining both strips to the wadding and backing fabric. Turn second strip to right side and continue in this way until the first half is complete. Return to the centre and make the second half. Work a line of stitches through the centre of each strip before trimming the edges and adding a separate binding.

Striped squares

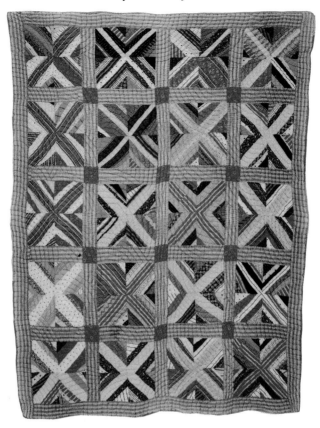

Early twentieth century American quilt. This uses a repeat of four squares set together and joined with lattice strips.

Materials A good scrap bag pattern providing an opportunity to use up oddments effectively. Choose contrasting colours for the lattice strips and squares.
Uses Use the pattern to make a cheerful everyday quilt.

Construction Cut a number of strips in varying widths and join diagonally to make a square. Make up three more squares and join together to make one block.

One block

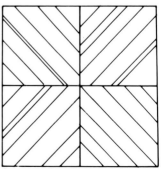

Cut a template the size of the smaller square plus seam allowance and trim all four squares to size before joining.

Lattice strips Lattice strips are an effective way of unifying a scrap quilt and reduce the amount of patchwork. Make two templates, one the width of the block, and a square template to make up the width of the lattice strip.

Alternate rows of blocks and strips of lattice with rows of lattice and square intersections. Sew all the rows together and add a separate border.

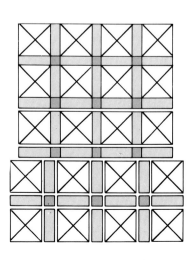

Diamonds II

A contemporary wall-hanging machine pieced and hand quilted, using a combination of commercial and home-dyed fabrics.

Materials Choose closely-woven cotton fabrics with minimum stretch for a pattern containing many small units, a number of which are cut on the bias. To obtain a deeper shade of colour dip fabric in a similar colour dye bath for a short time.
Uses Enlarge the basic pattern to suit either a bed quilt or a wall-hanging. Use smaller areas for cushions.

Construction Sew the pattern by machine or hand, using the backing paper technique. For machine sewing transfer the quarter repeat to graph paper making it the same size as the finished project. To make the templates copy each individual shape on to tracing paper, add a 6mm (¼in) seam allowance to each edge, stick on card and cut out. Cut all the patches and lay out the design. It is easier to make up the design in quarters but remember when cutting out to keep the templates right side up for two quarters but reverse them for the remaining two. For hand sewing transfer the complete design to graph paper, cut out each shape and use for backing papers.

One quarter of design

*Assemble the pattern in
horizontal strips or rows
then sew them together in
one piece.*

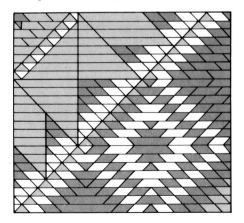

Seminole

A contemporary wall-hanging illustrating the strip technique developed by the Seminole Indians in southern Florida to decorate ceremonial clothing.

Materials Closely-woven dress-weight cottons in plain colours.
Uses Wall-hangings, quilts, borders or on a smaller scale for clothing decoration, bags and cushions.

Construction Follow the diagrams starting with the top band in the wall-hanging and working downwards 1-5.

Band 1

*Sew together four strips.
Cut into segments.
Reverse and join seg-
ments in pairs, then join
pairs offsetting one four-
patch square.
Trim top and bottom
band.*

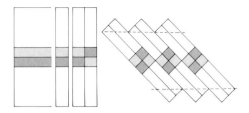

Band 2

*Sew together five strips.
Cut into segments.
Join together, offsetting
one square each time.
Trim top and bottom
band.*

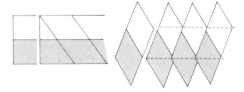

Band 3

*Sew together two strips.
Cut diagonally into seg-
ments.
Join together matching
points.
Trim top and bottom
band.*

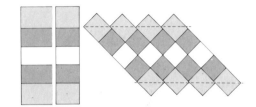

Band 4

*Sew together two strips.
Cut into segments.
Reverse, and offset seg-
ments before joining
together.
Trim top and bottom
band.*

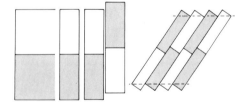

Band 5

*Sew together three strips.
Cut into segments.
Sew together two more
strips.
Cut into segments.
Join segments together.
Offset and sew together.
Trim top and bottom
band.*

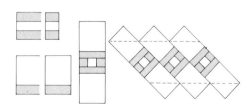

Manhattan

A contemporary patchwork coverlet that adapts the basic *Seminole* technique to create a colourful woven type design that is quick and easy to make.

Materials Choose a selection of colourful, plain cotton fabrics.
Uses The size of the overall pattern is most suited to a quilt or wall-hanging.

Construction This pattern is best made with a sewing machine. Select six colours, cut the fabrics into strips then join to make nine different lengths. Each length will be made up from a number of vertical strips of varying width. Cut the lengths into horizontal rows of equal width and reposition following the number on the right edge. Sew all the rows together. Add a separate backing and tuft the two layers together.

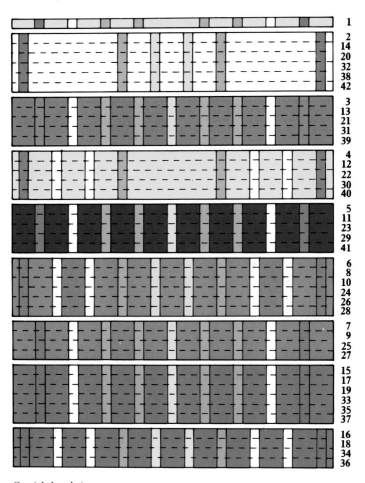

	1
	2 14 20 32 38 42
	3 13 21 31 39
	4 12 22 30 40
	5 11 23 29 41
	6 8 10 24 26 28
	7 9 25 27
	15 17 19 33 35 37
	16 18 34 36

*Cut eight lengths (one
length is just one row)
along the dotted lines
making a total of 42
rows. Reposition the
rows following the num-
ber on the right edge and
join to make one piece.*

REPEATED BLOCKS

The repeated block patterns
produce strong visual images which are characteristic of
American patchwork. They are exciting to use, and when
the blocks are set together, large overall designs are made
in which it is difficult to define the individual block.
Symbolic names were given to these patterns which
documented the lifestyle of the early settlers.
The older the block the more names
it collected.

Lady of the lake

American, Amish patchwork quilt 1930 This block originated in
Vermont after the publication of Sir Walter Scott's poem in 1810.

Materials Cotton is best for a pattern with so many small triangles. Use prints, or plain colours for a formal design.
Uses As a repeat pattern over a large quilt or hanging.

Construction Although the overall pattern appears complicated, the individual blocks are simple to make. Each small triangle must be accurately cut and sewn for the quarters to fit together. Give each block a quarter turn when setting them together.

Lady of the lake block

Make up each block in quarters by first joining the smaller triangles to each larger triangle. Piece the quarters into halves, then join together.

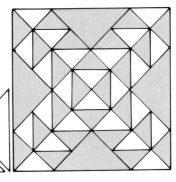

Churn dash

Nineteenth century American patchwork quilt The name derived from a typical occupation of the quiltmakers. Each block is set diagonally and joined together with large triangles.

Materials Use dress-weight cottons and make each block with different fabrics.

Uses Make one block for a bag, or join four together to make a large cushion.

Construction The pattern is quick and easy to make. Lay out the patches for one block. Sew the appropriate pairs of triangles and squares together and make into three rows. Sew the rows together.

Churn dash block

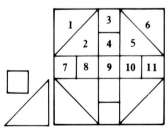

Join patches 1 and 2, 3 and 4, 5 and 6 together. Repeat for the third row. Join patches 7-11 together for the second row. Join all rows together.

Joining the blocks together

To join the blocks
together first make half
blocks to fill the top and
bottom edges on alternate
rows. Set the blocks
diagonally and join
together in vertical strips
with a large triangle in
between. Sew all the
rows together.

When making a half
block cut a separate set of
templates. Do not cut a
completed block as this
will not have the seam
allowances included on
the cut edge.

Nine-patch

Amish patchwork quilt 1920's
This quilt shows a pieced block set with plain squares.

Materials Choose brushed cotton in a plain colour which shows the stitches and is easy to quilt.
Uses The block is easy to sew and suitable for making a large quilt or wall hanging.

Construction To make a block first make the nine-patch units. Join the first row together nine-patch, strip nine-patch, then the second row: strip, square, strip and the third row: nine-patch, strip, nine-patch. Join rows together.

Nine-patch block

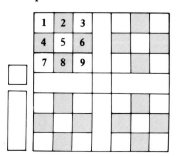

To make a nine-patch unit join patches 1-3, 4-6, and 7-9.

Setting blocks diagonally Setting pieced blocks with plain squares is a quick way to make a quilt.

When blocks are set diagonally with plain squares additional half and quarter squares are needed to complete the straight edges. Join the blocks and squares into diagonal rows then sew them together.

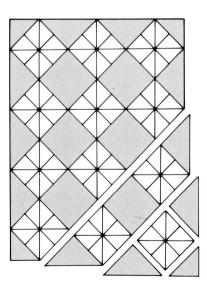

61

Garden maze

American patchwork quilt 1870 showing an unusual lattice-type design. Fine feather quilting patterns fill the plain squares.

Materials To minimize the amount of quilting, choose plain cotton fabric for the strips and a small print for the background. For a more extensively quilted patchwork reverse the placing of plain and printed fabrics as shown in the illustration.

Uses This pattern is best used as a repeated block on larger quilts, tablecloths or curtains.

Construction This block is basically made from equal width strips and worked from the centre outwards. It is easiest to first assemble all the patches and strips for one square and use it as a guide for the remaining blocks.

First join strips 1-4 to the centre square.
Then add triangles 5-8, followed by
strips 9-12. Make up the four corner
shapes, 13-15, 16-18, 19-21, 22-24.
Join one to each side to complete the
block.

Garden maze block

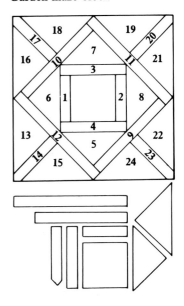

Dresden plate

A modern quilt using a pattern that combines patchwork, appliqué and quilting, it is also known as *Friendship Ring* or *Aster*.

Materials *The Dresden plate* is a good scrap bag pattern, each segment being made from a different fabric. Choose plain calico or cotton for the background squares.

Uses A popular pattern for a bed quilt, or use a single block for smaller articles such as cushions, table mats.

Construction To make one block first sew twenty segments into a plate shape. Appliqué four diamonds on to a small circle using the backing paper patchwork method, then sew this over the hole in the centre of the plate. Appliqué the completed plate to a background square.

Lattice Strips To make the strips join three narrow lengths of plain fabric together; use a print for the square intersections. Cut the pieced strips as long as the side of the block, join the blocks into rows with a strip in between and one at each end. Alternate these rows with strips of lattice joined with a square in between and at each end. Join all the rows.

Dresden plate block

Make a Dresden plate *template by folding a circle of paper into equal segments. Cut out one segment and round off the top.*

Border Use convex and concave edged shapes alternately for the border. Make up the border in strips and attach as for the straight cut border p.19. When the top and bottom strips are added carefully adjust the seam allowances so that the shapes turn the corner and lay flat. Add a separate binding to the edge.

MOSAIC

*Mosaic patterns are made up
from a repeated single geometric shape which is
usually a diamond, square, triangle, hexagon or octagon.
Some of the more intricate shapes are best sewn by hand using
the traditional English backing paper technique to create
an inlaid effect. Unlike most patchwork,
mosaic patterns are generally created by
a change of colour rather than shape.*

Sunshine and shadow

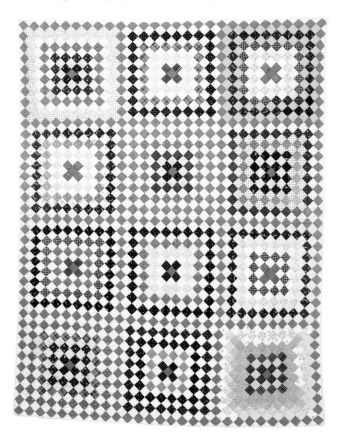

Nineteenth century American patchwork quilt A typical mosaic
pattern using squares that are set diagonally to make diamond shapes, it
is also known as *Trip around the world*.

Materials Use a selection of contrasting light and dark colours in small scale prints such as shirting fabrics. Avoid large prints that break up the regularity of the squares.

Uses A versatile pattern and good for beginners, it is suitable for quilts of all sizes, bags, cushions, tablecloths and clothes.

Construction Designs which use only one shape are confusing to put together so it is important to make a colour drawing of the design to use as a guide when sewing. Cut out all the patches, half shapes are needed to fill the edges and a quarter patch to complete each corner.

Join the squares together in diagonal rows, then sew to make one piece (see p.61).

Double axehead

American friendship quilt 1930s Each friend contributed a patch on which she embroidered her name. The friends then met to join the patches together and to quilt the patchwork. The quilts were usually made as a token of affection and presented to a parting member of the community.

Materials Choose a selection of cotton prints or plain fabrics and embroidery threads to make a friendship quilt. Closely-woven cottons have minimum stretch and are the best fabrics for curved seams.
Uses The *Double axehead* is a pattern that can be adapted to most items, but do not make the patches too small.

Construction For one-patch designs make several templates to avoid the edges becoming worn. Patches with curved edges require very careful cutting and piecing; if possible, cut with the long edge parallel to the selvedge of the fabric. Join the patches in rows. Ease the curves together with extra pins before sewing. Press the seams to one side, clip curves if necessary.

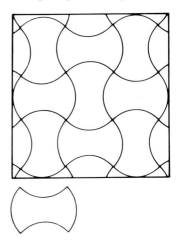

Alternate the position of each patch so that they interlock when joined together.

Setting the patches together

Diamonds

Nineteenth-century English patchwork coverlet has some of its backing papers and tacking stitches still evident. This patchwork records the richness and variety of fabrics available during that period.

Materials Choose good quality lightweight cottons or silk to retain the fine points of the diamond shape. Back slightly transparent fabrics with a light iron-on interfacing.

Uses Use this pattern for smaller scale projects; evening bag or spectacle case.

Construction Sew the diamonds by hand using backing papers. Use a wide diamond cut from isometric graph paper for the template. Make up the pattern from rectangular blocks of diamonds joined together with lines of single red diamonds.

Arrangement of diamonds

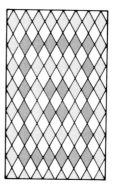

Start with a centre diamond and add one to each side. Continue in this way until the rectangle is complete.

Honeycomb

Nineteenth century patchwork quilt uses hexagons arranged in single rosettes. Although this shape is always associated with English work, it originated from the mosaic patterns of the Middle East.

Materials Use similar fabrics to those recommended for the diamond pattern. Choose a plain colour for the ground fabric.
Uses The hexagon is suitable for most items but it is usually hand sewn which is an important consideration when deciding what to make.

Construction For hand sewing hexagons see·p.18. To make one rosette join six hexagons clockwise around a central patch. Link the rosettes together with single patches.

Arrangement of hexagons

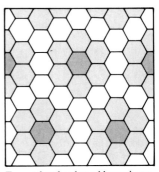

To complete the edges add part shapes, cover and sew in the usual way.

Squares

English wedding quilt 1850 made by Annie Heslop, of Northumberland. The patchwork top is made from multi-coloured chintz squares with a brown print border. The patchwork is elaborately quilted with a true lover's knot in the centre square.

Materials Printed chintzes, perhaps from a sample book
Uses A good beginners pattern and suitable for all sizes of quilts.

Construction Can be sewn by hand or machine. Start at the centre with the large square and add the smaller squares to all sides to make a progressively larger area. Half and quarter squares are needed to fill the edges and complete the corners.

Sew the squares into strips before joining to the main piece. Attach first the top and bottom strips, then one to each side.

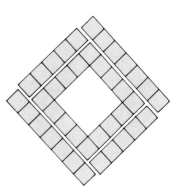

Octagons

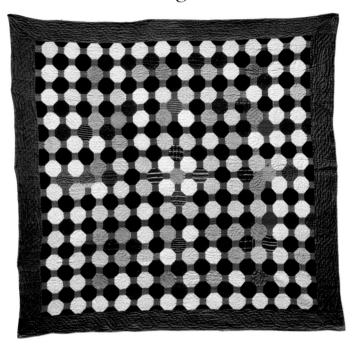

English patchwork quilt 1900 made by Sybil Heslop also of Northumberland. The quilt is made from flannels and suitings with a design of octagons on one side and large squares on the reverse.

Materials Use cotton fabrics for small patches or corduroys, flannel and suitings for larger shapes.
Uses The octagon and small square combination works well for utility quilts and lightweight floor rugs.

Construction If cotton fabrics are used, the octagon is a good shape to sew by hand using the backing paper technique. For heavier fabrics sew by machine.

Whatever the method of sewing, join the octagons and squares into rows, then join together. Add part shapes to complete the edges.

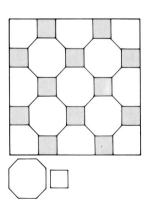

PICTORIAL

*Pictorial work is usually associated with appliqué
but pictorial patchwork can be made in several ways.
The most basic method is to build up an image from simple
shapes such as squares and triangles. Another way is to
simplify the subject into strips which are easy to piece
together. A third, more intricate technique uses
straight lined images made up from a number
of small pieces. The quilt below shows
an inlaid method, in which the patches
fit together like a jigsaw puzzle.*

Tailor's quilt

Mid-nineteenth-century Welsh quilt An extraordinary patchwork
quilt made by James Williams, master tailor of Denbighshire between
1842-52, it contains about four-and-a-half thousand patches and
besides depicting biblical scenes, records the achievements of the age.
The Menai suspension bridge is in the top left and the Ruabon Viaduct
in the lower half of the quilt.

You can't hide an army

A contemporary wall-hanging using an image that emerges from the background by change of colour. It is hand sewn using the backing paper technique.

Materials Choose closely-woven cotton fabrics in plain colours.
Uses Wall-hanging.

Construction Draw the design finished size on graph paper and make a smaller one for reference. Both drawings should have the patches numbered. Cut up the larger drawing and use the individual shapes for the backing paper technique (see p.18). Make up the design in rows, then sew together. Add a plain border.

Detail of head

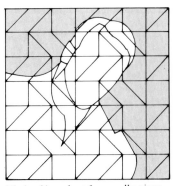

The head is made up from smaller pieces within the main shapes of the templates.

Elephant

A contemporary child's quilt showing an appealing circus elephant made in the simplest way from squares and triangles.

Materials Use plain cottons that show the quilting details for the sky and elephant, and choose small prints for the ground and decoration. It is especially important for children's items that the fabrics are washed and pre-shrunk.

Uses Child's quilt, wall-hanging or floor rug.

Construction Cut out all the pieces and arrange them in the correct order. Sew by machine or hand using a small running stitch. Sew into rows then sew these into one piece. Add a separate border.

It is unnecessary to make a full size drawing of the design but draw a small design on graph paper to work out the colours. Only two templates are needed, a square and a triangle.

Elephant design

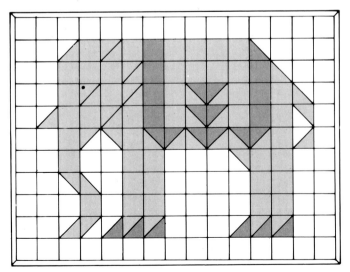

Butterfly

Contemporary patchwork wall-hanging machine pieced and quilted. Hand dyed fabrics have been used to achieve subtlety of colour.

Materials Use only closely-woven cotton fabrics.
Uses The large butterfly is complicated to piece together and more suited to experienced quiltmakers. Use the simpler block for smaller items or repeated on a bed quilt.

Construction Both the large and small butterfly block use the straight line technique which simplifies the image into smaller units for easier piecing. Draw the image finished size on graph paper, then make a template for each individual shape.

The heavier lines indicate the three main units for each half. Join patches 1-3, 4-8, and 9-12. Join together the two larger units then attach to the centre unit. Repeat for second half and join both together. Remember to reverse templates for mirror image.

Small butterfly

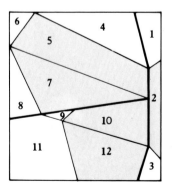

Large butterfly

The heavier lines indicate the eight main units for each half. First piece all the small patches together into each unit. Join units 1-3 and 4-6, join together.
Add unit 7, then unit 8. Repeat for second half reversing templates for mirror image.

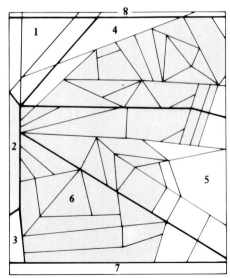

Sheep

A contemporary wall-hanging using a technique which simplifies an image into strips for easier piecing, which also makes it possible to add more details.

Materials Use only closely-woven cottons of similar weights in plain colours or small prints.
Uses Child's quilt, wall-hanging, or light-weight floor covering.

Construction Draw out the design finished size on graph paper, making the strips not less than 25mm wide. To make the templates, trace off each individual shape, add a 6mm seam allowance on all sides, stick on card and cut out. Number the shapes within the design and on each template for identification. Piece the design in vertical strips, most of which have several pieces and angled seams. Join the strips together to make one piece and add a plain border.

An alternative way to make the templates is to draw two designs to the finished size, use one for identification and cut one up to make the templates. Remember to number each shape for identification.

Sheep design

CONTEMPORARY

There has been renewed interest in quiltmaking
in recent years, with tradition inspiring exciting new
images and working techniques. Patchworks are made
to wear, display or sleep under, and also to express design
ideas. Some create strange optical illusions while others are
a series of more personal statements; for the latter no
instructions are given. If quiltmaking is to continue
and flourish it is important to make new statements
as well as to repeat traditional work.

Coat cover

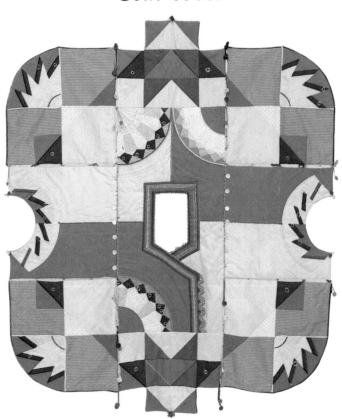

A reversible cloak (right side above) that can be worn, hung, or shown
flat, made from panels of patchwork, appliqué and quilting in silk and
cotton fabrics. The panels are joined with piping, buttons and tassels
(reverse side opposite).

Several themes and ideas led to the development of the coat cover, some of which had been the outcome of previous quilts which the maker wished to explore further. One idea was that of dividing the quilt into individual panels and finding ways to join them together. The theme of fans, their shape and structure, provided starting points for the patchwork patterns.

Cubic maze

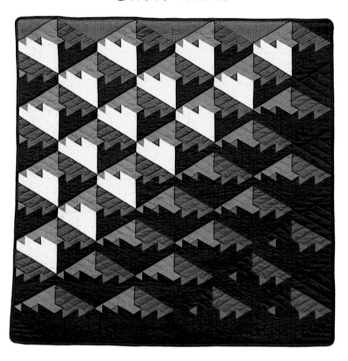

Machine pieced and quilted silk wall-hanging which explores the illusion of depth and three dimensional quality created by flat patterns and colours.

Materials Closely-woven plain cottons, or silk for brilliance of colour.
Uses Wall-hanging.

Construction The pattern is made from two different blocks, but with variation in colour.

Two blocks

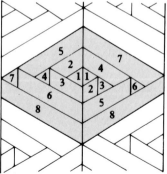

Join patches 1 - 8 in each block and piece together alternately in vertical strips.

Quilt of many cloths

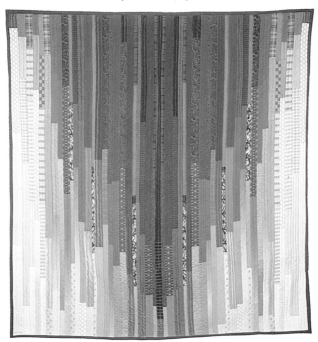

A contemporary wall-hanging intended for display in a large area. Machine-pieced and made from as many different fabrics as could be blended into one design.

Materials Satin, velvet, cotton, woollens and tweeds.
Uses The heavyweight fabrics and scale of design of this project make it suitable only for large items; wall-hanging, bed quilt or curtains.

Construction See technique p.47

Birds of paradise

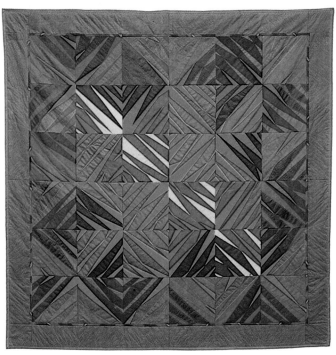

A modern wall-hanging machine pieced and quilted. Made from thirty-six blocks, each with a different design. The plain border is quilted with a similar pattern to that used in the patchwork.

Materials Closely-woven cottons in plain colours, filling of cotton domette.
Uses Wall-hanging or bed quilt.

Construction To make one block, draw out the design to its finished size on graph paper, stick on card and cut out the individual templates. Mark out each shape on the back of the fabric, add a 6mm (¼in) seam allowance and cut out. Sew all the patches together and press seams to one side. Cut a square of domette to the size of the patchwork block and machine quilt around the edge of each shape.

Completing the quilt Make up all the blocks and join together. Quilt lengths of fabric for the borders and attach using the separate corners method (see p.19). Add a separate backing and tuft the layers together at the corner points in each block.

Although each block is different, they follow a similar piecing sequence which avoids sewing into a corner. Join patches 1-15 and press seams to one side.

One block

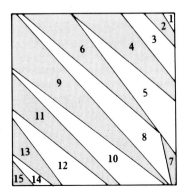

Stitched stripes

A series of experimental samples made in 1980, exploring the different patterns and textures made on the top and reverse side of patchwork. A variety of fabrics including silks, satins, synthetics and netting have been used, combined with hand and machine stitching. Postage stamps and magazines have been included as backing papers.

1 Postage stamp backing papers.
2 Raised textures made by seam allowances, machine stitched.
3 As 2, but using different shapes.
4 Strip piecing with fine ribbons and metallic fabrics.
5 Diagonal strip piecing.
6 Hand painted backing papers.
7 Seam allowances sewn flat around narrow strips of fabric.
8 Backing papers with hand written textures, contrast of top and reverse side.
9 Postage stamp backing papers.
10 Various fabrics stitched into diagonal strips.
11 Strip pieced triangles.
12 Reverse side including hexagons.

1	2	3
4	5	6
7	8	9
10	11	12

Mandala

Contemporary patchwork quilt machine pieced and hand quilted. The colours were inspired by the medieval stained glass in Chartres Cathedral.

Materials Dress-weight, pure cotton fabrics.
Uses Design intended for bed quilt or wall-hanging.

Construction The patchwork design is made up from four square blocks and three half blocks repeated throughout the design.

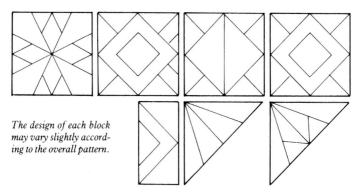

The design of each block may vary slightly according to the overall pattern.

One quarter repeat

The pattern is based on a square grid. The quarter repeat shows the position of each block. Additional diagonal lines have been added to frame the design.

Chequered cube

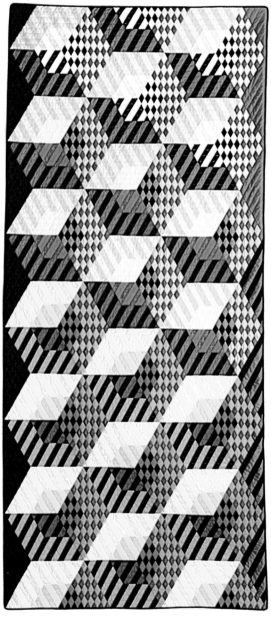

Top

A contemporary wall-hanging commissioned for a health centre. The design is based on the traditional *Tumbling blocks* pattern which has an illusionary three-dimensional quality.

Materials Closely-woven cottons in plain colours.
Uses Wall-hanging.

Construction The pattern is made up from two different blocks, repeated throughout but in different colours. Piece the blocks alternately into vertical strips then join together to complete.

To make the smaller block sew the thirty-six patches into eight progressively longer rows.

For the larger block make up in three main sections. First join strips 1-4 together. Next join the eight composite strips into one piece and finally join strips 21-24 together. Join all sections.

Small block

Large block

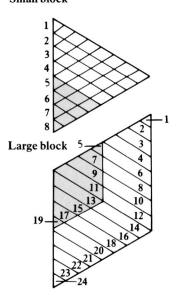

Colouring book

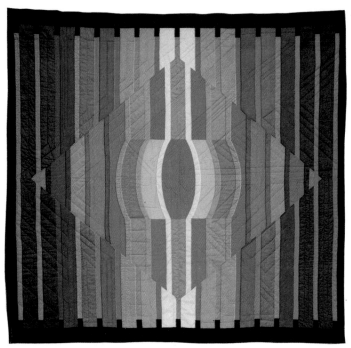

A contemporary patchwork quilt machine pieced and hand quilted.
The inspiration for the design came from a child's colouring book.

Index

A

Adding lattice strips 49
Adding plain squares 61
Appliqué 22

B

Basic techniques 7-19
    Italian quilting 12
    Patchwork 7, 13-19
    Trapunto quilting 12
    Wadded quilting 7-12
Borders 19

C

Contemporary 82-94
    Birds of paradise 86
    Chequered cube 92
    Coat cover 82
    Colouring book 94
    Cubic maze 84
    Mandala 90
    Quilt of many cloths 85
    Stitched stripes 88

D

Design
    Patchwork 13
    Quilting 8

E

Edging and lining 19
Equipment 7
Estimating the fabric,
   patchwork 16

F

Fabric 7
Filling
    for Italian quilting 12
    for Trapunto quilting 12
    for wadded quilting 7
Finishing 11

I

Italian quilting 12, 34-35
    Pastel squares 34

L

Log cabin 36-45
    Barn raising 40
    Chequerboard 36
    Courthouse steps 42
    Pineapple 44
    Straight furrow 38

M

Marking the fabric
    Patchwork 16
    Quilting 9
Mosaic 66-73
    Diamonds 70
    Double axehead 68
    Honeycomb 71
    Octagons 73
    Squares 72
    Sunshine and shadow 66

P

Patchwork
    Borders 19
    Choosing a pattern 13
    Design 13
    Edging and lining 19
    Estimating fabric 16
    Marking and cutting fabric 16
    Sewing 17
    Templates 14
Pictorial 74-81
    Butterfly 78
    Elephant 76
    Sheep 80
    Tailor's quilt 74
    You can't hide an army 75
Piping 11

Q

Quilting
    Cutting the layers 8
    Design 8
    Finishing 11
    Hand stitching 10
    Machine stitching 12
    Marking the fabric 9
    Using a frame 10
    Using a hoop 9

R
Repeated blocks 56-65
Churn dash 58
Dresden plate 64
Garden maze 62
Lady of the lake 56
Nine-patch 60

S
Sewing, patchwork 12-13
by hand 13
by machine 12
Sewing, quilting 10-12
by hand 10
by machine 12
Strip 46-55
Descent into tranquility 47
Diamonds II 50
Manhattan 54
Seminole 52
Striped squares 48
Strippy 46

T
Templates
Patchwork 14-16
Quilting 9
Trapunto 12, **32-33**
Flower garland 32
Tufting 11

W
Wadded quilting 20-31
Basket 22
Borders 26
Circles 25
Fans 25
Feathers 24
Filler patterns 26
Hearts 25
Leaves 24
North country 20
Repeated motifs 27
Shells 24
Wedding 28
Welsh 30
Wadding 7

Acknowledgments

Quilts reproduced by kind permission of
Beamish, North of England Open Air Museum 22, 46, 72, 73
The Bowes Museum 20
The Ealing Health Authority 92
Catrin Edwards-Jones 25
Mollie Evans 70, 71
Joanna Godfrey-Wood 48
Jane Kasmin 36, 38, 44, 56, 58, 66
National Museum of Wales (Welsh Folk Museum) 28, 30, 74
South East Arts 82
Michele Walker 24
Joen Zinni Lask 32, 60, 62, 68, 78

Quilts made by
Esther Barratt 88
Philippa Bergson 34
Joe Boyle 75
Margaret Brandebourg 40
Pauline Burbidge 78, 84, 92
Pamela Dempster 54
Janet Faulkner 52
Mary Fogg 47, 85
Lucy Goffin 82
Gillian Horn 94
Jenny Hutchinson 76
Francesca-Anne Kemble 90
Denise Orange 80
Sheila Scawen 42
Elizabeth Turner 64
Michele Walker 50, 86

Artists
John Hutchinson
Michele Walker

Photography
Ian O'Leary

Typesetting
Text Processing Limited

Reproduction
F E Burman Limited